The Atlas of the Seven Continents™

ANTARCTICA

Wendy Vierow

The Rosen Publishing Group's
PowerKids Press™
New York

For Chris, who loves atlases

Published in 2004 by The Rosen Publishing Group, Inc.
29 East 21st Street, New York, NY 10010

First Edition

Editor: Frances E. Ruffin
Book Design: Maria E. Melendez
Layout Design: Eric DePalo

Photo Credits: Cover and title page, Antarctic globe, p. 5 (world map), p. 19, 21 (Ross Ice Shelf, Antarctica) © Visible Earth/NASA; p. 5 (world map illustrations) by Maria Melendez; p. 9, 11, 13, 17 (Antarctic map) © GeoAtlas; p. 15 (Antarctic map illustration) by Eric DePalo; p. 17 (Antarctic Grass Clinging to Rock) © Peter Johnson/CORBIS; p. 17 (Emperor penguins) © Tim Davis/CORBIS; p. 17 (Crabeater Seal) © W. Perry Conway/CORBIS; p. 21 (Roald Amundsen and Crew) © CORBIS; p. 21 (Robert F. Scott) © Bettmann/CORBIS.

Vierow, Wendy.
Antarctica / Wendy Vierow.
    v. cm. — (The atlas of the seven continents)
Contents: Earth's continents and oceans — Antarctica long ago — How to read a map — A land of ice — Countries that claim Antarctica — The climate of Antarctica — Plants and animals of Antarctica — Natural resources of Antarctica — Exploring Antarctica — Scientists in Antarctica.
ISBN 0-8239-6688-7 (lib. bdg.)
1. Antarctica—Geography—Juvenile literature. 2. Antarctica—Maps for children. [1. Antarctica. 2. Antarctica—Maps.] I. Title.
G863 .V53 2004
919.8'9—dc21

                    2002154715

Manufactured in the United States of America

Contents

Earth's Continents and Oceans

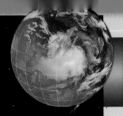

Antarctica is the only continent on Earth that is almost completely covered with ice. A continent is a large body of land. The seven continents on Earth are Africa, Antarctica, Asia, Australia, Europe, North America, and South America. As the fifth-largest continent, Antarctica is about 5,100,400 square miles (13,209,975 sq km). Only Europe and Australia are smaller than Antarctica. More than 200 million years ago, all the continents were part of a giant continent called Pangaea. Scientists think that the movement of Earth's plates caused Pangaea to break into smaller continents. Plates are huge pieces of Earth's **crust** that float on partly melted rock that is deep inside Earth. The movement of the plates caused Antarctica to move to the south. Today Earth's continents are still moving.

Long ago there was also one ocean, called Panthalassa. An ocean is a large body of salt water. Today there are four oceans on Earth. They are the Arctic, Atlantic, Indian, and Pacific Oceans. Some people call the water that surrounds Antarctica a fifth ocean, called the Antarctic Ocean or the Southern Ocean.

Arctic Ocean

Asia

Europe

North America

Atlantic Ocean

South America

Africa

Indian Ocean

Australia

Pacific Ocean

Antarctica

Equator

P A N G A E A

PERMIAN
286-245 million years ago

TRIASSIC
245-208 million years ago

Equator

JURASSIC
208-144 million years ago

Equator

The top map shows Earth as photographed from space. The maps below show what Earth might have looked like more than 200 million years ago. The continent of Antarctica in red, is shown breaking away from the giant continent, Pangaea.

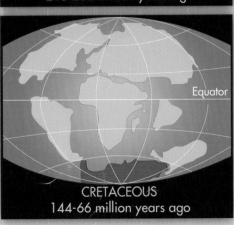

Equator

CRETACEOUS
144-66 million years ago

NORTH AMERICA

EUROPE   ASIA

AFRICA

Equator

SOUTH AMERICA

AUSTRALIA

ANTARCTICA

PRESENT DAY
From 66 million years ago

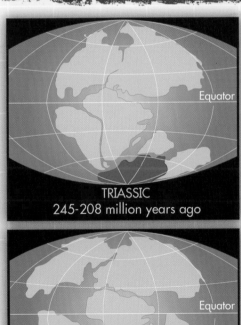
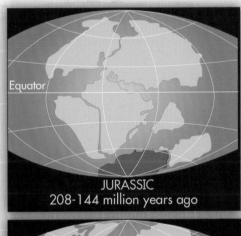

Antarctica Long Ago

During the Mesozoic **era**, which spanned from about 245 to 66 million years ago, Antarctica was a warm place, filled with plants and animals. The Mesozoic era was a time when dinosaurs and other reptiles were Earth's largest animals. Scientists learn about life long ago in Antarctica by studying fossils. The only named dinosaur found on Antarctica was the *Cryolophosaurus*, which was 26 feet (8 m) long. Fossils of a group of plant-eating dinosaurs called prosauropods, which *Cryolophosauruses* may have eaten, were found near the fossils of the *Cryolophosaurus*. In the air of Antarctica flew reptiles called pterosaurs. In the waters of Antarctica swam mosasaurs, or large meat-eating reptiles with four limbs shaped like paddles. Plesiosaurs, or reptiles with flippers, also swam in the water. Living near lakes and swamps was a mammal-like reptile called *Lystrosaurus*, which ate plants. There were many plants during the Mesozoic era, including Earth's first flowering plants. Other Mesozoic plants included ginkgo trees, conifers, or cone-bearing plants, and cycads, or trees that looked like palms or ferns.

This painting shows two cryolophosaurs, meat-eating dinosaurs that lived in Antarctica about 190 to 196 million years ago. They lived there when Antarctica was warm and covered with forests. A cryolophosaur was 20 feet (6 m) long. It is known as the *Elvisaurus*, because the crests on their foreheads resembled the hairstyle of Elvis Presley.

How to Read a Map

Maps have special features that help you to read them. You can find out the subject of a map by looking at its title. The title is often found in a box called the map key or the legend. This helpful box tells what the **symbols** on a map mean. To find out how distances on a map compare to distances of actual places on Earth, look at the map **scale**.

Most maps have a compass rose or north pointer that shows direction. The four main directions on Earth are north, south, east, and west. North is the direction toward the North Pole. Maps of Antarctica do not show a compass rose or north pointer because the South Pole is on Antarctica. All directions from the South Pole are north. All **longitude** lines meet at the South Pole and the North Pole. The **prime meridian** is 0° longitude. **Latitude** lines run from east to west. Latitude and longitude lines make it easy to find places on a map. The **equator**, which is 0° latitude, is the boundary line between the two **hemispheres** on Earth. The Northern Hemisphere is north of the equator, and the Southern Hemisphere is south of the equator.

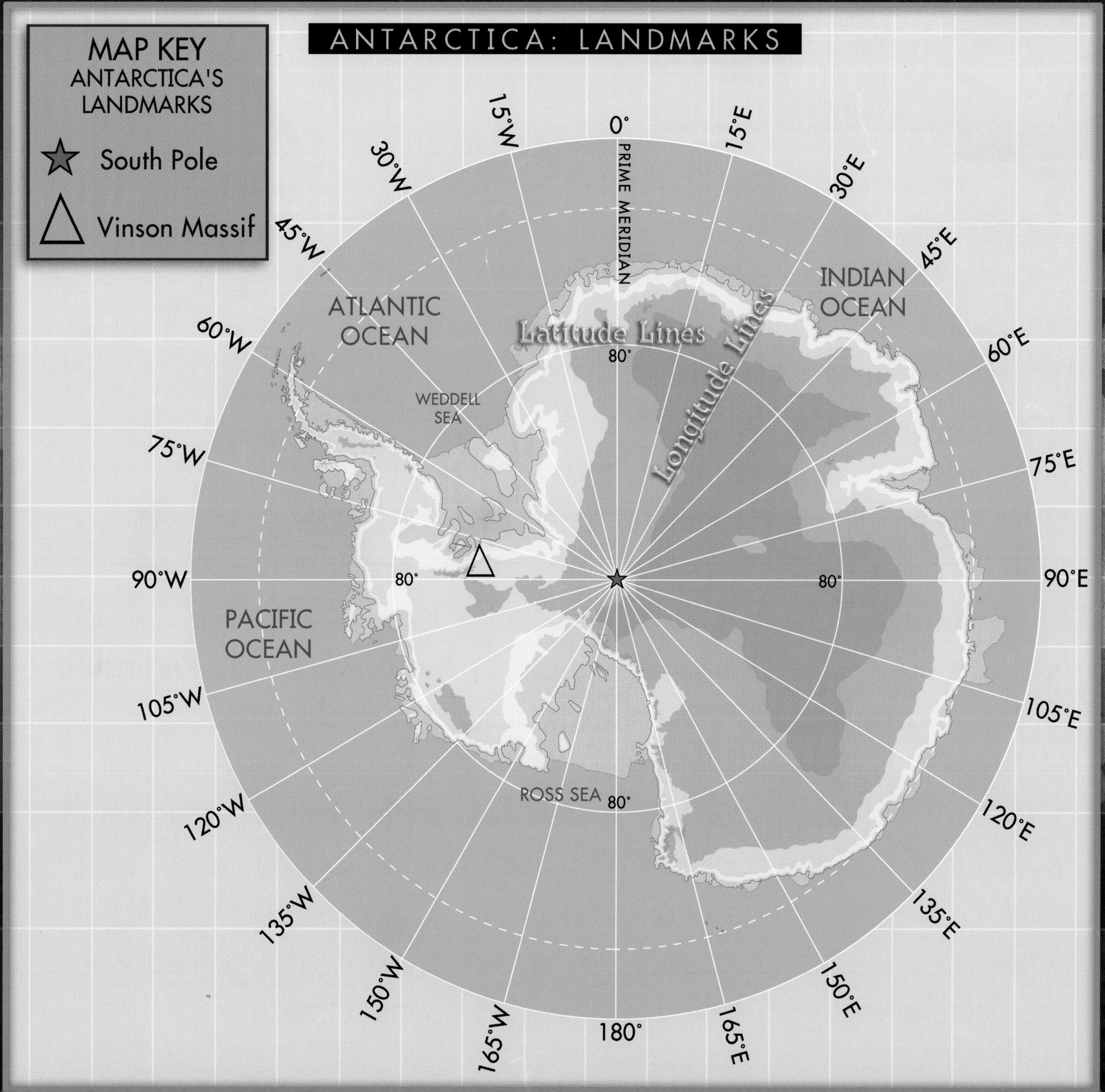

MAP KEY
ANTARCTICA'S
LANDMARKS

★ South Pole

△ Vinson Massif

15°W   0°   15°E

PRIME MERIDIAN

30°W   30°E

ATLANTIC
OCEAN

45°W   Latitude Lines   45°E

INDIAN
OCEAN

60°W   80°   60°E

Longitude Lines

WEDDELL
SEA

75°W   75°E

90°W   80°   80°   90°E

PACIFIC
OCEAN

105°W   105°E

120°W   120°E

ROSS SEA   80°

135°W   135°E

150°W   150°E

165°W   180°   165°E

A Land of Ice

This satellite view shows a crack in the ice caused by the melting of the Larsen Ice Shelf in Antarctica.

Today about 98 percent of Antarctica lies beneath an **ice cap**. Underneath the ice, which is almost 3 miles (5 km) deep in some places, are different **landforms**. The Transantarctic Mountains cross Antarctica, dividing it into East Antarctica and West Antarctica. Along the coast of East Antarctica are **glaciers**, mountains, and valleys. Most of Antarctica is a desert because it has so little **precipitation**. West Antarctica has volcanoes, including Antarctica's most active volcano, Mount Erebus. West Antarctica also includes the Antarctic **Peninsula** and its nearby islands. Near the peninsula, in the Ellsworth Mountains, is Antarctica's highest mountain, the Vinson Massif, at 14,067 feet (4,288 m). The Bentley **Subglacial Trench**, which is the lowest place on the continent at 8,366 feet (2,550 m) below sea level, or the average level of the ocean's surface, is also in West Antarctica. This trench is about the size of Mexico and is filled with ice. **Ice shelves** float in the oceans around Antarctica.

ANTARCTICA: LAND AND WATER

15°W
30°W
45°W
60°W
75°W
90°W
105°W
120°W
135°W
150°W
165°W
180°
0° PRIME MERIDIAN
15°E
30°E
45°E
60°E
75°E
90°E
105°E
120°E
135°E
150°E
165°E

South Orkney Islands

ATLANTIC OCEAN

Fimbul Ice Shelf

Riiser-Larsen Peninsula

Riiser-Larsen Ice Shelf

Antarctic Peninsula

WEDDELL SEA

Coats Land

Queen Maud Land

Enderby Land

INDIAN OCEAN

South Shetland Islands

Larsen Ice Shelf

Graham Land

Palmer Land

Mount Jackson

Ronne Ice Shelf

Valkyrie Dome

Lambert Glacier

Mackenzie Bay
Amery Ice Shelf

Alexander Island

East Antarctica

American Highland

West Ice Shelf

BELLINGSHAUSEN SEA

Ellsworth Land

Transantarctic Mountains

POLAR PLATEAU

80°

PACIFIC OCEAN

Ellsworth Mountains

West Antarctica

Shackleton Ice Shelf

AMUNDSEN SEA

Bentley Subglacial Trench

Wilkes Land

Marie Byrd Land

Getz Ice Shelf

Queen Maud Mts

Ross Ice Shelf

Roosevelt Island

Taylor Glacier

Mount Erebus

80°

Ross Island

Victoria Land

Talos Dome

ROSS SEA

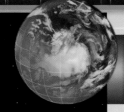

Countries That Claim Antarctica

Although Antarctica doesn't have any countries, seven countries claim land in Antarctica. These countries are Argentina, Australia, Chile, France, the United Kingdom, New Zealand, and Norway. By 1961, 12 countries, including the United States, had signed the Antarctic **Treaty**, which states that Antarctica can be used only for peaceful and scientific reasons. By 2000, 15 more countries had joined the treaty, and 18 other countries had agreed to follow the treaty. The map on the next page shows major **research** stations run by some of the members of the Antarctic Treaty. Under the Antarctic Treaty, scientists who work in Antarctica must share the results of their studies about Earth's **environment** and about the universe.

The largest research station in Antarctica is McMurdo Station, run by the United States. During the summer, which has constant daylight, about 1,000 people stay at McMurdo Station. However, during the dark winter days, which in the Antarctic last from May through August, about 250 people stay there.

ANTARCTICA: LAND CLAIMS

15°W
0°
15°E
30°W
30°E
45°W
45°E
60°W
60°E
75°W
75°E
90°W
90°E
105°W
105°E
120°W
120°E
135°W
135°E
150°W
150°E
165°W
165°E
180°

PRIME MERIDIAN

Norway Claim

Neumayer (Germany)
Maitri (India)
Novolazarevskaya (Russian Fed.)
Orcadas (Argentina)
Aboa (Finland)
Sanae (South Africa)
Troll (Norway)
Syowa (Japan)
United Kingdom Claim
Argentina Claim
Chile Claim
Halley (U.K.)
Belgrano II (Argentina)
Molodezhnaya (Russian Fed.)
Dome Fuji (Japan)
Mawson (Australia)
Progress (Russian Fed.)
Zhongshan (China)
Davis (Australia)
Chile
Patriot Hills (Chile)
Amundsen-Scott South Pole (U.S.A.)
80°
80°
80°
East Antarctica
West Antarctica
Mirnyy (Russian Fed.)
Vostok (Russian Fed.)
Australia Claim
Unclaimed
Casey (Australia)
Scott Base (New Zealand)
Dome Concordia (France and Italy)
McMurdo (U.S.A.)
80°
Terra Nova Bay (Italy)
Dumont d'Urville (France)
France Claim
New Zealand Claim

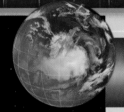

The Climate of Antarctica

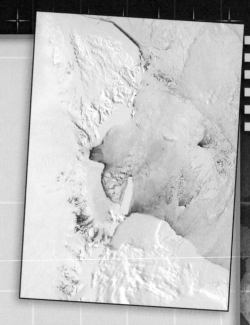

This is a satellite view of the Ross Ice Shelf, taken from space to show the location of new icebergs.

Antarctica, the coldest place in the world, has a polar ice cap climate with freezing **temperatures**. In addition to being the coldest place in the world, Antarctica is also one of the driest. This is because the air is too cold to hold moisture. Antarctica is so cold and dry that its climate resembles the climate of Mars!

Many things affect climate. Climate includes temperature and precipitation. Places near large bodies of water have cooler temperatures in summer and warmer temperatures in winter than inland places. Along the Antarctic coast, the climate is milder with more moisture than the climate in the middle of the continent, which is cold and dry. In the summer month of January, temperatures on the coast may reach 32°F (0°C), compared to inland temperatures of 5°F–31°F (-15°C– -0.56°C). Along the coast there is an average of 24 inches (61 cm) of precipitation annually, while inland there are only about 2 inches (5 cm) of snow each year.

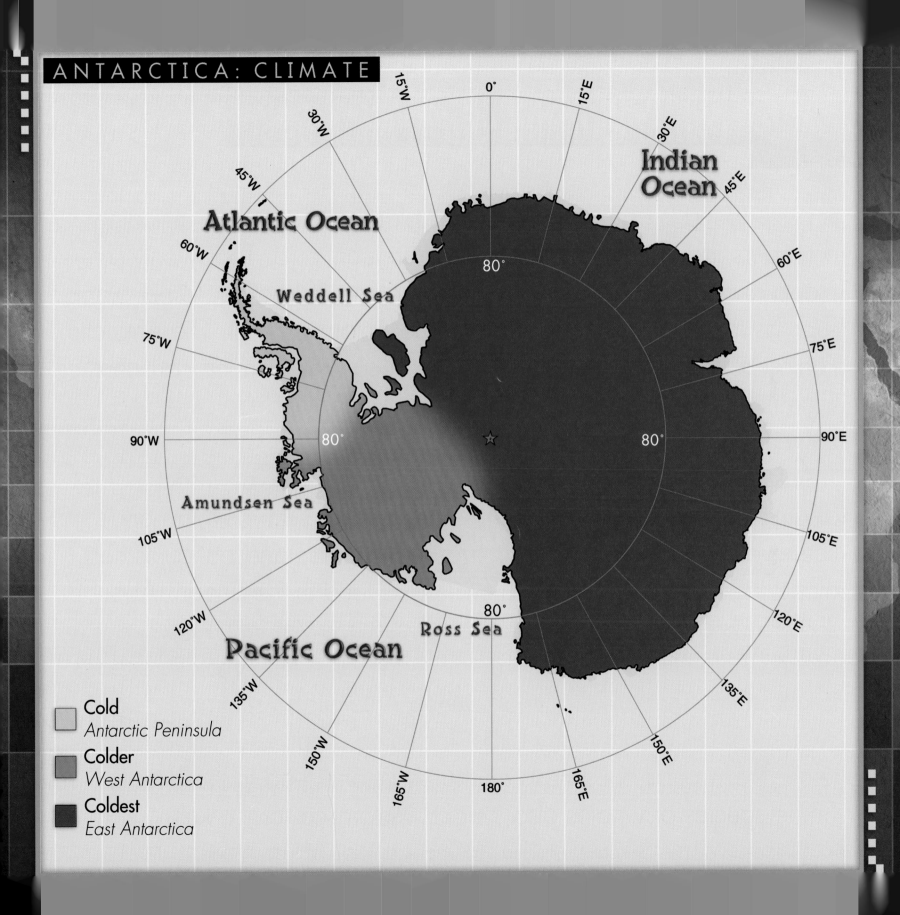

ANTARCTICA: CLIMATE

15°W · 0° · 15°E · 30°W · 30°E · 45°W · 45°E

Indian Ocean

Atlantic Ocean

60°W · 60°E

Weddell Sea

75°W · 75°E

80° · 80°

90°W · 80° · 80° · 90°E

Amundsen Sea

105°W · 105°E

120°W · 120°E

Pacific Ocean

Ross Sea · 80°

135°W · 135°E

150°W · 150°E

165°W · 180° · 165°E

Cold
Antarctic Peninsula

Colder
West Antarctica

Coldest
East Antarctica

Plants and Animals of Antarctica

Fossils found by scientists show that plants and animals, including dinosaurs, lived in Antarctica millions of years ago. Today only a few plants and insects live in the inner part of icy Antarctica. Other plants, such as mosses, grow mostly along the Antarctic coast. The Antarctic Peninsula is home to the only two flowering plants on the continent. One is a grass called *Deschampsia antarctica* and the other is a flowering plant called *Colobenthos subulatus*.

Antarctica's largest animal is the wingless midge, an insect that is about ½ inch (12 mm) in length. Other insects, such as mites and lice, live on ocean animals, such as seals. Seals and penguins nest along the Antarctic coast, and swim and feed in the ocean. About 120 kinds of fish, including cod and icefish, swim in the oceans around Antarctica. The most common animal in the Antarctic oceans is krill, a tiny shrimplike animal. During Antarctica's summers, huge swarms of krill attract many birds, including albatrosses, gulls, and terns. These birds build nests on the coast and feed in the ocean. Some **species** of whales also swim to Antarctica for the krill.

Antarctic grass clings to a rock on the Antarctic Peninsula.

Emperor penguins are the world's largest penguins. They can grow 4 feet (1.2 m) tall.

This crabeater seal relaxes on a piece of pack ice. Crabeater seals often live alone, but sometimes can be found in groups of about 1,000 seals. They can dive 98 feet (30 m) into the ocean for their food.

75°W
90°W
105°W
120°W
135°W
150°W
15°W
75°E
90°E
105°E

Antarctic Peninsula
East Antarctica
Transantarctic Mountain
South Pole
West Antarctica

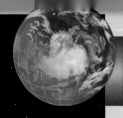

Natural Resources of Antarctica

Antarctica has other natural **resources** besides plants and animals. Many **minerals**, including copper, iron, and gold, lie under Antarctica's ice cap. Coal can be found in the Transantarctic Mountains. It is also possible that oil lies in the Ross Sea and the Bransfield **Strait**, although icebergs and rough seas would make drilling difficult. Most of Antarctica's minerals occur in amounts too small to make them worth mining. Mining is not allowed under the Antarctic Treaty. Many people believe that mining will hurt the environment in Antarctica.

An important natural resource in Antarctica is freshwater. Antarctica's ice holds 70 percent of the world's freshwater. If scientists could find a way to use Antarctica's freshwater, people in many parts of the world that have poor water supplies could be helped. One suggestion is to tow icebergs to places in the world that need water. Some icebergs are very large. The largest iceberg ever seen was found near Antarctica in 1956. At 208 miles (335 km) long and 60 miles (97 km) wide, it was about the size of Belgium!

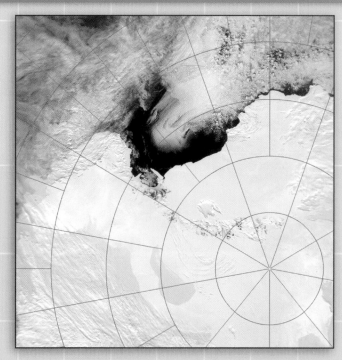

Above: This view of Earth from space shows the Lambert Glacier. It is the world's largest glacier, which might be a source of freshwater.

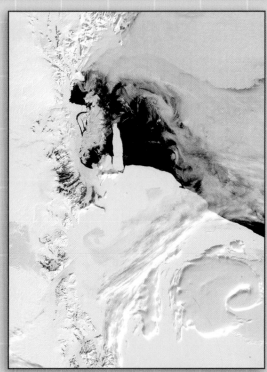

A photo from space shows Victoria Land, in the Ross Sea and the Ross Ice Shelf, the world's largest ice shelf.

Above: This picture, taken from high above Earth, shows the South Pole and the Ross Sea, where oil might be found.

Exploring Antarctica

The ancient Greeks believed that there was a southern continent long before people ever saw Antarctica. One of the first people to explore the area near Antarctica was James Cook from England. In 1772 and 1773, he sailed toward Antarctica, but could not reach it because ocean ice blocked his way. The first sighting of the continent was probably by either Russian navy captain Fabian von Bellingshausen, British navy captain Edward Bransfield, or an American seal hunter named Nathaniel Brown Palmer. All these men sailed to Antarctica in 1820. The first known landing at Antarctica was in 1895, by a Norwegian ship searching for whales.

One of the most famous events in Antarctica was the race to the South Pole. Norwegian Roald Amundsen and British captain Robert Scott set out in 1911 to reach the South Pole. Amundsen and his four assistants reached the South Pole on December 14, 1911, a little more than a month before Scott's group arrived. Amundsen's group made it through the journey alive. However, Scott and his four assistants died on the return trip.

Capt. Amundsen and his Crew on board the "GJØA" Nome, Sept 1st 1906

Captain Robert Scott skied at the South Pole.

Explorer Roald Amundsen was photographed with a crew of men as they sailed through North America on a water route called the Northwest Passage. The photo was taken five years before Amundsen sailed to Antarctica and reached the South Pole.

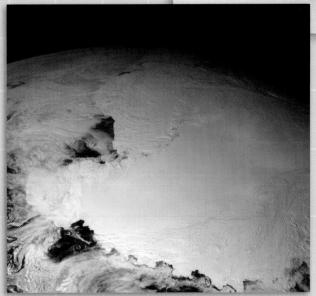

The curve of planet Earth was photographed from high in space. The photo also shows the outline of the continent of Antarctica.

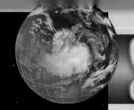

Scientists in Antarctica

Many scientists study global warming in Antarctica. Global warming is an increase in Earth's temperature. Global warming causes climate changes that could result in sea levels rising because of melting polar ice. In 2002, British and American scientists saw a part of Antarctica's ice shelf, about the size of the state of Rhode Island, break up over 35 days. They believe warmer temperatures destroyed it. If more ice shelves fall apart because of warmer weather, the sea level could rise. This would cause places around the world with low elevations to flood or to disappear underwater.

American Sarah Gille of Scripps Institute of Oceanography at the University of California in San Diego led a study to find out the temperature of the ocean around Antarctica. Gille compared water temperature readings gathered over the past 50 years. The results showed that the ocean around Antarctica is warming twice as fast as oceans in other parts of the world. If the ocean warming continues, the sea ice around Antarctica will become thinner and will break up, causing sea levels to rise worldwide.

Glossary

crust (KRUST) The outer, or top, layer of a planet.

environment (en-VY-urn-ment) All the living things and conditions of a place.

equator (ih-KWAY-tur) An imaginary line around the middle of Earth that separates it into two parts, northern and southern.

era (ER-uh) A period of time or history.

glaciers (GLAY-shurz) Large masses of ice that move down a mountain or along a valley.

hemispheres (HEH-muh-sfeerz) The halves of Earth or another sphere.

ice cap (EYES KAP) A huge layer of ice and snow that covers a large area of land.

ice shelves (EYES SHELVZ) Wide, flat sheets of an ice cap that float on water.

landforms (LAND-formz) Features on Earth's surface, such as a hill or a valley.

latitude (LA-tih-tood) The distance north or south of the equator, measured by degrees.

longitude (LON-jih-tood) The distance east or west of the prime meridian, measured by degrees.

minerals (MIH-ner-ulz) Natural elements that are not animals, plants, or other living things.

peninsula (peh-NIN-suh-luh) An area of land surrounded by water on three sides.

precipitation (preh-sih-pih-TAY-shun) Any moisture that falls from the sky.

prime meridian (PRYM meh-RIH-dee-en) The imaginary line that passes through Greenwich, England, and that is 0° longitude.

research (REE-serch) Having to do with study.

resources (REE-sors-es) A supply or source of energy or useful materials.

scale (SKAYL) The measurements on a map compared to actual measurements on Earth.

species (SPEE-sheez) A single kind of plant or animal.

strait (STRAYT) A narrow waterway connecting two larger bodies of water.

subglacial (sub-GLAY-shul) Referring to the area at the bottom of a glacier.

symbols (SIM-bulz) Objects or designs that stand for something else.

temperatures (TEM-pruh-cherz) How hot or cold things are.

treaty (TREE-tee) An official agreement, signed and agreed upon by each party.

trench (TRENCH) A deep crack in the ocean floor.

Index

Web Sites

Due to the changing nature of Internet links, PowerKids Press has developed an online list of Web sites related to the subject of this book. This site is updated regularly. Please use this link to access the list: www.powerkidslinks.com/asc/antarct/